T0128773

PTSD

NATIONAL HOMES FOR HEROES/ SPIRIT HORSE II

The Lighter side, if in fact there is one

ELIZABETH WILEY MA JD, POMO ELDER
TRAINER, AND EQIUNE THERAPY DIRECTOR

Order this book online at www.trafford.com
or email orders@trafford.com

Most Trafford titles are also available at major online book retailers.

Print information available on the last page.

ISBN: 978-1-4907-9344-3 (sc)
ISBN: 978-1-4907-9348-1 (e)

Trafford rev. 01/25/2019

 www.trafford.com

North America & international
toll-free: 1 888 232 4444 (USA & Canada)
fax: 812 355 4082

NEVER forget good music: it helps heal. Even a sob story song if used properly can help you let go the bad and recover. I like those country western, treated me bad, there is the door, and I am not going to look in the rear view mirror type songs….. DOWN THE ROAD SHE WENT….my Dad used to love that saying, when the world kicks you, get up and head on down the road to something better!

DEDICATION

TO ALL THOSE who suffer this mysterious and often deadly disease.

TO ALL THOSE who have broken themselves in attempting to find the key to help the sufferers heal.

TO the FAMILIES and friends of those who suffer

TO all those in MY family who have suffered from the antics of those who suffered from PTSD and yet continued to love those afflicted, no matter that they could not feel safe around them, and had to restrict their contact.

TO MY MOM for her work with PTSD combat soldiers, to all those she healed, to the families she reunited, or helped build extended family support to live the best they could, separated due to unhealed PTSD. For the comfort she gave to those with PTSD and to the families and friends of those who were not able to make it back through the dense horrors that harmed their lives.

TO MY SONS who have been the love, the inspiration for my life and work. I had my older son, and realized, in the horror of the Vietnam War, and that never ending draft that made it obvious I was raising my two precious babies to finish high school, be drafted and in country in whatever war the great "they" had involved us in before the summer was over. Along with our own history of Rez genocidal, a Native California Pomo history, I sure had a nerve to inflict life on them. SO, I got involved in helping this word be a better place. More on that later.

TO MY "Riders' we do NOT label our program participants, no one knows who is a staff member, volunteer, or "rider". We call them ALL riders. There are TWO books and soon to be two new ones on those programs (Carousel Horse is our inclusion working program book, with a screenplay to help those "riders" who can not, or are not allowed to come to the stable, Spirit Horse II is the first book for our teaching manuals for those who want to share their horse, or dog, or cat, or bird, or any other animal with anyone to help this world heal). Our programs are for high risk youth, veterans, first responders, and their families, and others (divorcing families, those with terminal illnesses and critical care staff, nurses and doctors).

THANK you to TIM G. WILEY for his allowing us to use the photographs he sent to you as chosen by the lay out department. The pictures are all nature, pets, etc, to inspire our class participants to learn to enjoy and be grateful for all the world gives to us, rather than be limited by material items they do not have, or have found themselves to be dissatisfied with when they have managed to get them.

ALL I WANT FOR CHRISTMAS IS YOU

As discussed in the introduction to this book, it is often hard for a sufferer of PTSD to realize how much their pain, suffering, and confusion is hurting those who love them, and those who need them to love them in return.

Your children, parents, sisters, brothers and friends are heartbroken at holidays, your birthday, THEIR birthday when you are not there. Not able to find your way out of whatever your particular hell is.

Crosby, Stills, Nash and Young once wrote a song that had a line that said, "Teach your children well, YOUR private hell, will slowly go by". I think of it so often when hosting a mediation or facilitating a negotiation for child custody or divorce. How wonderful if we could all learn to deal with our own private hell, to resolve the issues, and pass along the ability to be happy, joyfilled, grateful for the good things of life, and to SEE them, and for the strength and wisdom to get through the bad times.

This is not about making a PTSD sufferer feel guilty, it is NOT about blaming the PTSD sufferer, it IS about working hard, with the millions of other PTSD sufferers, to heal yourself, to allow others to help you heal, and to recognize and help those you have harmed while suffering to heal. It is about one day, when you have healed, to pass along the help and support to others who are suffering.

I was listening to seasonal music on my cable station, and ALL I WANT FOR CHRISTMAS IS YOU came on. I remembered instantly Christmas after Christmas when my only wish was to have the return of the person I loved. My Dad, my husbands, my brothers, nephews, friends lost in PTSD. I now realize My Mom as well.

Over the years my friends, loves, Dad, brothers, nephews and sons have recovered and gone on living their lives, My Mom. It took me many decades to realize that she too had PTSD, never treated. My Mother was a Berkeley PhD researcher at the San Francisco Presidio with the Commander of Psychiatric studies to address what they after World War II called "Battle Fatigue". She had been an Army Red Cross Nurse doing work with returning hospitalized combat soldiers. WHAT!

My Mom was a concert level piano player, she had been the Choir Director for a famous Episcopal children's choir. She could make costumes, design and work with scenery and back drops. She could integrate the children's art into each project. She was an amazing dancer, and loved the USO dances held to say good bye to deploying troops, or returning troops in the San Francisco area bases and for the injured soldiers at the Presidio social services because, amazing woman that she was, she had her THIRD masters degree in Psychology and earned her MSW to become a licensed social worker to work in family services before the war, and during and after the war in her research fellowship at the Presidio, as part of her PhD program for Berkeley.

She painted pictures that could have hung in galleries and collections of very wealthy people. She could sew, cook, and had been a Girl Scout Troop leader for foster children and community troops for kids who had parents that could NOT be leaders due to felony arrests, even though at the time she did not have children. She volunteered and helped young women who had no families, or families that would NEVER recover from their own PTSD, and accompanying addictions caused by many things, racism, war, police work, nurses, doctors.

It occurs to me that maybe the reason DOCTORS formed the first Alcoholics Anonymous because THEY themselves realized THEY needed to heal and save their own lives was because doctors, and many others have real lives NONE Of us could survive without addictions, and they recognized the reality. Many of their peers committed suicide by alcohol, drugs, sex addiction that led to divorce from their loved ones, and behavior that often alienated their family and friends and colleagues. We have only to watch an episode or ten of MASH to see how the doctors were destroyed by the massive in country horror they were drafted and forced to deal with. Alcohol and drugs.

HOW did my MOM become a person who led herself into the deepest of the horrors of what people can do to others, themselves, and the earth itself?

As I thought, and began to notice how many of the high risk youth I worked with were related in one or more ways to veterans, who obviously had PTSD, often decades before it was called PTSD, and who were broken by the broken condition of their relative or friend.

Maybe her own family veterans, Dad, brother, foster brothers, Uncles, so many others led her to understand the sadness, anger, and often danger, to themselves and their own family members as well as others that came from what today is titled PTSD. She and her family members were also First Responders.

Her Mother lived through the horror of a young daughter who died a slow and soul shaking leukemia. She died at thirteen. There were no treatments or hope for leukemia in the early 1900's. My Mom never recovered from the suffering and death of her sister. One day the tiny, shrunken girl asked my Mom if she was going to go to the angels. My Mom said "OH, of course not, God will not take you". When she passed away, so did my Mother's faith in God. None of us realized that until decades later when my Uncle told us that my Mom had never been the same again after her sister died. She felt she had prayed, and God had not answered her prayers. (more on the subject of God and PTSD below). BUT she took us to not just her church for Sunday School, but also to the churches of my Uncles on the Rez who were Assembly of God ministers, and to the Native American conferences, then called Festivals, in our own language, today called Pow Wows She took us to celebrations of every religion held in the homes, Temples, Mosques of her college friends. She taught us to respect the belief systems of others as well as our own. Even though she had lost her faith due to her sister's death, she kept faith in God to pass to her children.

GROWING UP WITH PTSD

All eight of the children in our family three of my Mom's children, and five of my Step Mother's children, due to BOTH Mother and Father suffering from what one day would be known as PTSD, grew up with the side effects of PTSD.

Today we know what it is, but the treatment is not available to those who need it. I was told by a Marine Corps Commander in charge of programs that they had plenty of great, successful programs, but "you can lead a horse to water". I said, this is a lucky day, I am a horse trainer, and I was taught, you may not be able to MAKE a horse drink, but if you make a horse thirsty enough, it will drink".

ALL Veteran programs and those for active duty soldiers are failing most of the soldiers and veterans.

The best programs are over booked and can not take new patients, or the reality that once a person admits to PTSD they are closed from many professions or may lose their own jobs makes it hard for those who are able to find an opening to get into the best programs. Many of the other programs are NOT good programs.

LAUGHTER, the best Medicine:

Jokes are often about sad, horrific, and tragic situations. The stories put in this book to make people laugh are intended to heal, not harm.

I love lawyer jokes, and religious jokes. They are not meant to be against, or sacrilegious, they just make us think, and hopefully laugh.

A young woman noticed her room mate struggling with a huge ham. She hacked at it until she cut it to allow a small part of the ham go into one pan, the rest of the ham into another pan, and put the two pans into their large oven.

Why are you doing all that work asked the young woman.

The room mate answered, "Because that is how my Mother always did it". Case closed.

One day the young woman was out shopping with the Mother of the roommate, and remembered to ask her about the ham and why it was cooked that way. The Mother looked surprised and said, OH, because my Mother always cooked a ham that way. It is the only way to cook a ham. The room mate wisely kept it to herself that her family put a ham in a pan and cooked it over all her young years.

When the roommate invited her to a family celebration, she met the Grandmother, and asked her kindly, why their family cut the ham and cooked it in two pans. The Grandmother looked surprised and said I have no idea why they do it, but when I got married, we lived in a tiny apartment with a tiny stove we bought as our first family gift to each other. I could not fit a whole ham in that little oven, so I cut it and cooked part, then cooked the second part. Until our youngest child went to college, we kept that tiny stove.

Think about this story. Think about what it means to PTSD and to relatives, friends and co-workers of people suffering from unrelieved PTSD.

What might you be doing in life because "that is the way it is done". Many first responders, and military or veterans have learned a hyper vigilant lifestyle, and easily get overwhelmed watching life too carefully. Most of the rest of the people are not nearly as stressed, because they are unaware.

Write some thoughts on this page.

Some people that have patrolled dangerous combat war zones have trouble balancing their lives back upon return to "normal" community life.

Write some thoughts about your day and see if this is an issue for you, or someone you care deeply for, who appears stressed or is beginning to refuse to go to stores, parties, or public places.

Research some self help books that might help you deal. Talk to other veterans, and some of the VFW, or other veteran group members, it will help when you realize how many others have the same feelings and issues.

One Vietnam era Marine told us when he came back he had some serious problems with his thoughts on his own sanity. He snarled at his family and felt very stressed at work. He heard other veterans had horses and dogs, and it helped them calm down. He got a couple of horses, and shared them with his family, but he also learned over time, and shared with other veterans, that when he felt stressed, or as if he was becoming short with the family, he would say, well, time to give the horses a bath, or clean stalls, or go feed the horses. His family learned to say, in a calm manner, GEE Dad, you think the horses need their bath, or hay, or their stall cleaned. They had found a way to communicate with love and understanding and he learned that even if he had to clean every stall in the stable, for all the owners who were grateful to share the chore, he could wear down and work out in his mind his stress and anxiety. After a ride, or grooming the horses, he felt relaxed and came home ready to be the husband and Dad he wanted to be, not the one he sometimes had trouble controlling.

One of our friends had bought his daughters a horse, but when they went away to college, he had to begin to take care of her, he wanted to keep her for his very young daughter who lived with their mother, they were divorcing. One day, after having himself cleaned stalls for others, and his own horse, he said.... NOW I get it, I know what you all meant when you said you would rather come down here and clean s)@#(*$t than to go home and take it.

This thought was echoed by many divorcing women over the years, and by college students coming up on examinations. Many of them had no interest in riding, they said the horses just made them feel relaxed, grooming them, or cleaning the stalls. The other boarders at the stable did not ever complain!

One supervisor for a huge project used to come and groom the horses out in the full hot sun, bringing carrots and treats for them. We always asked if she wanted to ride. She replied always, WHAT, do you think I am crazy.

Until she moved away, she let go of the stress of her day when work was just too much, by bringing treats and grooming horses in the sun.

Several people came to groom or work with the K-9 Therapy Dogs, or work in the vegetable garden. We had several seniors who just liked to come and sit in the sun, or shade, and bring carrots and other treats for the horses, and treats for the dogs, goats, chickens, ducks, and bunnies, pigeons and wild ravens. They also listened to many of our high risk youth, veterans and first responders. Just listened. While listening they taught those young people to calm down and be part of the calm of the animals and the day.

What can you think of to help yourself get a balance routine?

Laughter: The Best Medicine

One day a man swam too far out in bad tides, and began to drown.

A lifeguard saw him, and got his board, his lifeguard station floatee, with its bright painted Red Cross, and swam out to the man.

The man said, "OH NO, GOD is going to save me" and waved the lifeguard away.

A boater saw the man and also attempted to help him, throwing him the lifesaving ring from the boat, the man pushed it away and shouted, "OH NO, GOD is going to save me".

The man drifted farther out to sea. A Coastguard Cutter came and attempted to help him, he waved them off and said "OH NO, GOD is going to help me".

Finally a helicopter with police officers came and attempted to capture him and take him to safety. He fought them off. And drowned.

At the pearly gates, he glared at Gabriel and said, "I trusted GOD, how come he did not save me".

Gabriel said, "He sent a life guard, a boater, the Coastguard and a rescue helicopter what more did you want".

Think about this joke.

In what ways do YOU fail to take help that is available to you.

LOVE is one of the greatest life saving means GOD gives to us. What can you do to make those who love you, and those you love more able to save your from your PTSD?

This is NOT about blaming a person with PTSD, it is about overcoming the PTSD itself and getting help. As the saying often goes, NO ONE can do your pushups for you, and NO ONE can reach out and get help when PTSD has a grip on you.

NOT FUNNY:

One of the greatest problems with PTSD is that it is NOT treated like a broken leg, or concussion.

Many jobs or careers will not allow their employees or members to be HUMAN and have a really reasonable reaction to extreme emotional, physical and mental trauma……..

Whether citizens who have been robbed, raped, mugged on the street, or in an accident that caused their PTSD, or the often violent deaths of family or friends, or veterans, first responders, or high risk youth who have never had the opportunity to build their solid self base to balance and support them in their young lives, whatever has happened that has thrown them off………they are often put on medications and labeled, NOT helped.

Veterans and First Responders and Critical care staff live more trauma in a day than most people have in an entire lifetime. We have been begged to give them some form of relief, because over and over we have been told, they have begged their Unions, their stations, their supervisors to build a supportive program. There have been a few pilots, but they were not continued. One was very successful, it was a simple as a couple of weekend events for family and friends; both on duty, and off duty members were asked to attend.

The result was that the groups seemed to just have a powerful relieving effect on everyone. The children and spouses realized they were NOT the only ones who had to deal with someone who had so much to deal with on some days, going home and taking a shower and going to bed seemed too much to ask, let alone to parent, and be a partner.

These groups began to have formal pamphlets, videos, and presentations on how others were dealing with issues.

Like the Marine veteran who worked out his horses needing care as a signal, each family needs to talk honestly and learn their own ways of coping.

IF there were programs that did NOT reflect on the career or job of the active duty, first responders, and critical care personnel, such as police dispatchers and air traffic controllers, and other high stress positions that often put the workers looking at the worst situations humanity can think of many times a day.......they would go to them.

Seeing a therapist AFTER they have gone too far, and been fired, or suspended makes the situation harder to deal with.

In our groups, no one signs in, no one talks about others, like Court mandated domestic violence groups, the members are asked to NOT gossip, or to mention to others in the group outside of the group that they know each other. A police officer, fireperson, or paramedic, doctor, nurse or other high stress job person who is greeted by another member runs the risk of a co-worker or supervisor asking HOW DO YOU KNOW THAT PERSON.

This is counter productive to training people how to deal with the realities of their day to day jobs.

EXERPTS from :

Therapeutic Horsemanship for Women Active Duty and Combat Veterans who have been Sexually Assaulted during service.

This is an inclusion book. An inclusion book is a book that was written with the help of those who are to use the book for educational and healing purposes. In this case, women combat and combat area support service veterans who have been sexually assaulted in active duty areas. Many of the women veterans involved in therapeutic horsemanship in many different programs have added their thoughts and input to this book. The second part of the book is a screenplay. In inclusion work, it often helps group members to read and then comment on parts of a script that include the issues and thoughts of those who have been involved in similar programs. Doing the parts also helps members of programs to address issues within themselves from an anonymous standpoint of being the actor.

While no one person IS a real person, many of the members of the riding programs, meditation, sweat lodge, and other programs have similar thoughts and issues after having survived combat and / or being sexually assaulted in active duty areas.

DISCLAIMER: This book and screenplay are total works of fiction. NO PART of either the story, or the screenplay is about one identifiable person, place or event.

There are many therapeutic horsemanship programs across this nation, many of them run at no, or low cost by horse owners with care, love and concern for our veterans and their families.

NONE of the material is about one identifiable program, event or person.

At current time the women veteran's book is not published for public use, but the materials are used in groups, of equine, K-9, Animal Assisted and other programs of self help for women veterans. The book is scheduled to be published in late 2019.

Spirit Horse II, while compiled with several volunteer Psychiatrists, and consulting neurologists and therapists, is a self help program using the healing of animals. We do NOT use our animals as substitute couches for our "riders". No one knows, except the Directors which people are volunteers, paid staff, consulting professionals, or veterans, first responders or high risk youth and their families.

While many of our "riders" staff and Directors as well as volunteers participate in groups or private therapy programs, they are separate from the equine therapy programs. We believe horses, dogs and other animals heal, and it is our job to let them do their job.

Only staff, volunteers, and professional consultants certified in Spirit Horse II programs is allowed to work in the programs. Training staff, volunteers or professional consultants often are in the program, but are identified by the insignia on their shirts as trainees, or consulting professionals in training.

A large part of our program consists of volunteer group projects. While working with others, on one of our own projects, or community programs the members are given time to talk to others and realize they are NOT the only ones. We volunteer groups in local VFW, American Legion and other veteran group projects just for the reason that the veterans will meet older veterans and find out they are not even the "only" or the "first" generation to have, or overcome PTSD and other problems veterans often face.

We suggest each of our program participants find large group volunteer projects and share them with others in the group. One of those often attended are Habit for Humanity projects and fundraiser. We found early on that groups of veterans, no matter what age, have an inner well trained, get it done mentality that makes them amazing. One of our projects was moving out stable from one site to another. We thought it would take about three weeks. Working with volunteer groups on the weekends, and doing as much as possible each day with our own volunteers and staff.

We were fortunate to have a Veteran Center social worker who had a large group of veterans that needed something fun, yet purposeful to do. One of our volunteers was a retired Marine Sergeant. He picked up the moving van sized rental truck, tools, and all the veterans had been asked to bring tools to help. In three hours they had broken down all the stalls, arenas, and sheds, and packed up all the office, tackrooms and moved them in two truckloads to the new location and re-assembled them. Our Director went and bought them all breakfast and we sat around and chatted about a news story that obviously had ALL of them tense, because once it came up, the tension was relieved.

We realized, and our Marine Sergeant told us, that military are used to pulling down work areas, hospitals, and air support bases to move them and put them back up as fast as possible. WE were certainly convinced.

Twelve Steps Back From Betrayal

This is a quasi Twelve Step book. We are in process of finding out how to create an authorized 12 Step program.

The process of meetings is similar.

Step One

I admit that my life is out of my control. That the act (s) of betrayal by those I had to trust to have my best interest at heart while in a combat zone left me with an out of control and unsafe feeling I am not able to dispel. I am powerless over the feelings of anxiety, fear, anger and despair that overcome me.

Step Two

I come to believe that there is a power higher than me that can take control over my life and restore me to peace of mind, heart and soul.

Step Three

Made a decision to turn myself over to that power for care of God as I understand God to be.

Step Four

Took a searching and fearless journey into my experiences with the knowledge of the Higher Power being beside and surrounding me for protection.

Step Five

Admitted to God and to others the reality of my fear, depression, anger, hatred and anxiety that has overtaken my life. This step is not about reliving the assault. This step is about how the fear, depression, anger, hatred and anxiety are harming my life and the lives of those I love.

Step Six

Became entirely ready to turn the whole of these experiences and their consequences on my life today over to God for His disposal

Step Seven

Humbly Asked God to remove all the doubt, anxiety, fear, hatred, self loathing, anger and feelings of being out of control and unsafe. Humbly Asked God to protect me and made a decision to trust God to give me the courage to trust again.

Step Eight

Made a list of all those persons I am harming, including myself, by refusing to let GO, and let God take over the experiences, the emotions and my continuance of the overpowering of my life of these betrayals.

Made a list of all those persons, even the unknown ones, and what it is that I have to learn to forgive them for. What I have to learn to let GO and let GOD deal with to give myself the gift of freedom from these past experiences. This is not about saying it is all right what others have done, this is a step of releasing the fear, anxiety, anger, depression, rage that I have kept welled inside of me. I learn that forgiveness is for ME, not the person (s) I am forgiving.

Step Nine

Made direct amends to those I have harmed, where it will not harm them further, including myself, by my actions due to the overpowering fear, anxiety, anger, hatred I have had dominate my life since the betrayal(s).

Step Ten

Continue each day to keep a daily personal inventory of my set backs in reliving and allowing these past experiences to steal the joy and love from each current day of my life

No one is perfect. When tired, or stressed I may fall back into flashbacks and anxiety, fear, anger, I will learn to exercise my strength within to help me let each one go, and not begin to build a new burden of negativity related to horror that is in the past.

Step Eleven

Learned to utilize prayer and meditation to improve my constant contact with God as I know God to be, and to use that growing knowledge to help me keep the past behind, and the future a positive thought, not a negative fear filled anxious one and live today in gratitude for the presence and protection of God as I understand God to be.

Step Twelve

Having gotten the gift of a new and growing peace of mind, heart and soul as a result of others sharing their journey with me, I will share my journey with others to help them find the healing presence of God, as each understands God to be, and to learn these Steps and pass them to others who suffer from Betrayal by Brothers in Arms.

By learning the principles I have been given a clean slate, I learn to share that clean slate with others by teaching and living these principles as an example of the Grace of God as each of us individually understands God to be.

Laughter: The best medicine

A man every time the lottery was held, watched carefully on the news to see if anyone had won.

Every time he asked GOD, how come I never win.

Week after week, he complained, and looked to GOD saying HOW COME I NEVER WIN

GOD are you against me?

One night, the sky lit up, and a voice thundered into his home: BUY A TICKET!

Sometimes we complain, blame, whine, and get depressed. Winning the lottery is a very small chance, the news people said the last big lottery it was 1 chance out of 300 MILLION that anyone would win.

BUT, a man was walking his dog, the dog was sniffing at a piece of paper, the man went to take it from the dog, and it was a couple of dollars folded up and dirty. He walked on and saw the lottery sign in the window of a market. He bought the dog a ticket. THAT DOG won the whole, huge lottery pay out. Of course the man won the money, but he was clear he meant the dog to have great benefits for its whole life. He had never bought a lottery ticket before!

SOMEONE has to win. BUT, it makes no sense to spend your rent or mortgage or car payment on lottery tickets. ONE ticket wins.

I personally was at the pet store, and noticed a liquor store next door that had a lottery sign, the pay out was big, and I realized that our work pool had not collected for that week. I bought a ticket. I won over $800 for a partial number ticket. I split it with the people in our pool, because I had bought it for the pool. The pool decided to give me the $20 I had spent on the ticket back.

Over the years I have occasionally bought a ticket, and have won a few, lost a few, and always am thankful and think it is fun.

One day at the track my sister Leona and I were jumping up and down, two little old ladies, because our horse had come in. A man nearby said, WOW, how much did you win? We looked at the sign and said, OH, $2.17 or something, we had paid $2 for the ticket. The man smiled and said, I would hate to see it if you won the lottery, you would probably drop over dead from a heart attack.

Buy a ticket. You never know.

BUT look for the things that are likely to help you with life, there are many people and things that can help you, but not if you do not buy a ticket.

A ticket might be talking to the older vets, or to your siblings, or to a therapist who is on a crisis hotline and not allowed to ask you any personal information.

Write down some "tickets' that might help you.

Twelve Steps Home from war

This is a quasi Twelve Step book. We are in process of finding out how to create an authorized 12 Step program.

The process of meetings is similar.

Step One

I admit that war has caused my life to be out of my control. I am powerless over the feelings of anxiety, fear, anger, guilt, sorrow and despair that overcome me.

Step Two

I come to believe that there is a power higher than me that can take control over my life and restore me to peace of mind, heart and soul.

I have come to believe that God, as I understand God to be, brings the sun up each day, forgiving all of humanity for our acts and failures to act that grieve God as I understand God to be.

I have come to believe that God, as I understand God to be, forgives and loves me no matter what I have done, or seen done.

I have come to believe that God, as I understand God to be, allows me to find that forgiveness for those who have harmed me.

I have come to believe that God, as I understand God to be, welcomes me with open arms, a concept I may have stopped believing I am worthy of receiving.

Step Three

Made a decision to turn myself over to a higher power for care of God as I have come to understand God to be.

Step Four

Took a searching and fearless journey into my experiences in war with the knowledge of the Higher Power being beside and surrounding me for protection.

This is a sponsor driven Step. The work may be done with a therapist, in group therapy as I find the best position for myself to overcome my life as it has been and begin to shape my life as I want it to be.

This does not necessarily mean to relive every moment and horror of war. It means that as I work with my sponsor, therapists, and friends, family and other members of this program I will find a path away from the reality of what I have lived through. I will learn how to release the feelings, and memories that are binding me to that experience and become freed to a now, and a future of joy, serenity and love.

Step Five

Admitted to God and to others the reality of my fear, guilt, depression, anger, hatred and anxiety that has overtaken my life.

Whether to a therapist, a sponsor, or a group, I relate to myself and another how my life has changed and the emotions deep within that are keeping me from enjoying and being grateful for my life. Denial is a reality that may be shielding me from my own self destruction. I will discuss this with my therapist, my sponsor, my group as I see fit.

Step Six

Became entirely ready to turn the whole of these experiences over to God for His disposal

Step Seven

Humbly Asked God to remove all the doubt, guilt, anxiety, fear, hatred, self loathing, anger and feelings of being out of control and unsafe.

Humbly Asked God to protect me and made a decision to trust God to give me the courage to trust again.

Step Eight

Made a list of all those persons I am harming, including myself, by refusing to let GO, and let God take over the experiences, the emotions and my continuance of the overpowering of my life of these feelings, actions emotions.

Made a list of all those persons, even the unknown ones, and what it is that I have to learn to forgive myself and others for.

I will have to learn to let GO and let GOD deal with each item on this list to give myself the gift of freedom from these past experiences.

This is a sponsor driven step. I will work with my sponsor, my therapists, family, friends, and other program members to work this step.

Step Nine

Made direct amends, where possible, and where it will not cause further harm to those I have harmed, including myself, by my actions due to the overpowering fear, anxiety, anger, hatred I have had dominate my life since the betrayal (s).

Step Ten

Continue each day to keep a daily personal inventory of my set backs in reliving and allowing these past experiences to steal the joy and love from each current day of my life

No one is perfect. Some days are easier than others. Learning to let go, and be with life in a joyous and current moment way is not always easy. This moment I can choose to recognize my humanity and let go of set backs and enjoy and love in today.

Step Eleven

Learned to utilize prayer and meditation to improve my constant contact with God as I know God to be, and to use that growing knowledge to help me keep the past behind, and live today in gratitude for the presence and protection of God, as I understand God to be.

I will utilize prayer and meditation to improve my trust in the future and release the anxiety and watchfulness that harm me and those who love me by keeping me away from a serenity filled, joyful moment today.

Step Twelve

Having gotten the gift of a new and growing peace of mind, heart and soul as a result of others sharing their journey with me, I will share my journey with others to help them find the healing presence of God, as each understands God to be, and to learn these Steps and pass them to others who suffer from being unable to come home from war.

By learning the principles I have been given a clean slate, I learn to share that clean slate with others by teaching and living these principles as an example of the Grace of God as each of us individually understands God to be.

THIS IS A DRAFT of an article for handouts from veteran street programs: Suicide from the Inside:

At the Oscars, on stage, accepting his award, the world needs to thank Graham Moore, for acknowledging his own teen depression and suicide experiences. We need to seriously understand that many of the veterans committing suicide are barely beyond their teens. In a class I have been taking on building and rebuilding dreams after traumatic illness, injury or serious economic reversals, several of the class members admitted to having attempted, or been seriously close to suicide when they had failures and losses in family, business, and personal life goals, but were now for the first time sharing that depth of their personal despair and reality. I admit to having cut my wrists at sixteen, with the war, the draft, losing almost SEVEN HUNDRED older brothers of friends, who died, came back with what today is called PTSD, or were maimed over a two year period to Vietnam, and realizing that I would never marry, and that our world was in a seemingly unending mess of war, hate and unhappiness, I just thought I would find peace, instead I woke up with a bloody mess to clean up before anyone else woke up, and feeling weak and dizzy, but knowing I wanted a better world, not to be dead.

I wrote a paper, based on statistics we had studied from the front page of the newspaper for a math class, our advanced theories math teacher had asked us to bring in front pages of newspapers, and we chose an article and he demonstrated on the board statistics and how they are created. When he got to a certain statistic, he said, this can NOT be, either mathematics is wrong, or the article is not correct. His reasoning? Either by statistics the Vietnamese were asking each American if they were related to someone in our math class, at our high school, in our city, and if so, killing them, letting the others go, OR, the numbers in the paper were not correct.

My paper was on the theory of the paper not giving us the truth. I got an A for composition, an F for content because the English teacher was for the war. I was so angry I moped. That C average lowered my grade and I was hoping to be the first Native

American woman at Stanford and go to law school, that C would make sure I did not make that dream come true. I decided this world was just too drear for me. I can still remember looking out the window and seeing a brown tinted world, and just slashing my wrists, I had considered how to get out the fastest and easiest way. I just thought I would find peace

SUICIDE is a very terminal solution to what may not be a terminal problem.

IAVA in a recent e-newsletter stated that the current statistics are showing 22 veterans each and every day commits suicide. The reasons listed have been many in articles on the same subject. Lack of care, PTSD, sexual assaults while in active duty, depression, lack of job, loss of family, and failure of the VA to establish programs for the veterans who know full well if they do expose themselves for suicidal thoughts, they will be labeled, given psychotropic medications and lose their last chance for reaching their dreams, since the careers they have in mind are closed to those who have a history of mental illness and/or of taking psychotropic medications.

While volunteering in a phone bank at our large urban city political campaign center, our Director and I mentioned the work we do, and the findings we had heard at the recent Military Families Conference we had attended, which had ended with a conclusion that the greatest numbers of veterans are refusing to ask for help because they do not want to be labeled mentally ill. One of the center Directors said, I wish I had known you were there, you keep up that work. We had said we do not get funded, but the groups that do provide a list of centers that will help free, and they are all overwhelmed. Most do not get funded because they take and keep no information, which is why the veterans come in the first place, since they are afraid to be labeled as mentally ill, or are in denial of the true level of their problem. She said her son had come home from the war, seemed happy to be home, started to college, and putting his life together. He went with a group of friends to an out of town weekend, and without a word to any of his family or friends, walked off a high-rise hotel rooftop.

SUICIDE is a very terminal solution to what may not be a terminal problem.

Everyone in the room stopped, mid word on the phone banks, and we all just teared up. In veteran volunteer projects we deal with this story on a daily basis. Parents, spouses, friends wanting to know what they did wrong, and how to help the family and friends deal with the loss. Others who say they can feel it coming, in a withdrawal of the veteran or active duty friend, or family member that can not be pinned down, but is felt, and they do not know how to deal with helping.

One commenter on an internet news story last week wrote that in his opinion it was just old vets, not the young returning from Afghanistan and Iraq, and other places where they are deployed recently that are committing suicide.

He is mistaken, no one really has adequate statistics, or care to research them regarding the statistics for the old veterans. Down in the wash where we rode our horses, we saw a police officer. The lady I was riding with asked him if they had identified the body some riders had found a few days before.

He said "body?" and proceeded to tell us that someone died there at least once each day, and most were older veterans living in those homeless camps along twenty miles of river and wash beds under the bridges.

The veterans that the recent article was talking about are the young, recently returned veterans, they are the ones the statistics are relating the 22 suicides a day upon, not old veterans that are not even counted as suicides, even though years of addiction and exposure have been a slow form of self death.

One veteran told me, shortly before he disappeared, and I later was told he was killed in a freeway accident, that he wanted me to pray for him, because God did not want to hear from him any more. Since then I have heard many other veterans express the same thought. I steer them to military chaplains, who are certainly more qualified than I to deal with both God and severely lost young veterans. I want to say that having worked with gang abatement programs, and criminal rehabilitation programs, as well as domestic violence Court Mandated programs as a volunteer for decades, veterans are not the only ones who have somehow gotten the idea that God does not want to hear from them and has turned His back on them. I do not believe God, or a Higher Power, ever turns against us, or does not want to hear from us. Having worked with criminals for most of my adult life, I do not think God, or a Higher Power turns against any of us for our faults, or acts, or not acting as we need to. NO MATTER WHAT.

The thought of a peaceful somewhere is not limited to one time in life:

I spoke to my Dad, and he said "sometimes the "s.....t" is so high, its up to your eyes, and you need a straw to breathe, but just keep on walking, and one day, you will find the sun shining, and things are getting better". My Dad was a Native American paratrooper dropped behind enemy lines into Germany, and was shot. He could not connect with his unit, and spent some years living on his reservation learned survival skills while he managed on one leg to drag himself to France and finally find an American unit to rescue him. His hair was so long that when the General saw him, he asked my Dad, how could someone who looks so much like a little girl have been such a good combat soldier. Some of his unit had turned him in for posthumous awards, thinking he had been killed in action. His hair had grown that long since his military haircut and having been dropped behind enemy lines! Being a Native American, he was sure his brown little face would bring instant death should he ask for help from the enemy.

We then created another special quasi Twelve Step based on his program for Women Veterans who have been sexually assaulted or harassed while in active duty, named "Twelve Steps Home from Betrayal by Your Brothers at Arms". These programs were donated free to the military and veteran chaplains to be posted on websites and able to be utilized as self-help FREE. They will be posted free on a new website as well soon. We wrote and asked the 12 Step Anonymous program if we could do that, they said just email them a copy of our material. We did, and they did not tell us to stop. I was told as long as we say quasi.....we can use a step format to help ourselves and others heal.

It did not matter, if I over ate, drank, took drugs, over spent, was addicted to gossip, or housecleaning, or exercising, shopping, plastic surgery, or work, if what I was doing was keeping me from complete responsibility for my own happiness and life, I was addicted and needed the help offered.

There are more than one way to commit suicide and hurt those who love us right along with ourselves.

SUICIDE is a very terminal solution to what may not be a terminal problem.

I also spoke to a friend of mine who was a doctor, I wondered if I was just nuts. He said "anyone who ever tells you they NEVER considered stepping over the edge is a liar, everyone has times when it is so horrible, painful, hopeless and overwhelming think that there might be peace somewhere, but we have to do the things necessary to not do it". It made me feel better just to know that my Dad and my learned friend thought it was OK to think about it, but to find a better way of dealing.

Another friend, a doctor from the ER where we worked was talking to a suicidal patient, he said, "is there any way I can help talk you out of this?" The person said "no". He said, then I will have to call professionals to help you, and called the police to transport the person to the 72 hour hold at the mental hospital. He told the man, someone has to help you, and they are the professionals. I am just a doctor paid to save your life. I remembered that when family and friends came to me and told me they were in fear of their loved persons life, or even their own life.

One disabled friend recently called the police on herself, and spent a 72 hour hold in which she learned she had a very horrible, tough situation, being foreclosed out of a house someone had forged and fraudulently tricked her out of her HUD loans for disabled people and sticking her with a predatory loan on a falling down house. Ten years of fighting it and she lost to corruption, not even to her own acts. The hospital helped her realize that NO MATTER WHAT that house was not worth dying over, and neither was her belief that America would never let a disabled person be treated this way. Obviously, she learned in that mental hospital, it would, and that was not worth dying for either. The judge had just said, this is going on too long, I am going to put a stop to this. The Constitution guarantees her a jury trial before losing property, but that judge did not even give her a chance to present her evidence to a jury.

SUICIDE is a very terminal solution to what may not be a terminal problem.

I read a letter to the helpful advisor of national paper syndicated column in which a woman said she was thinking of suicide because of anger and hurt over a lot of things. The columnist wrote that she might try confronting each person that hurt or angered her, and if she did not feel she could talk face to face with them, write a letter describing the feelings. I did not read the part, until years later when the column was re-run in a book, that said throw out the letter. I mailed them if the person refused to talk. Soon, I was really able to put thoughts in order and discuss them, and find a better way in life than let people harm my joy and peace. A friend of mine said during her divorce, she started a mediation class looking for a new career. She found in the mediation training process a way to deal with her own failure to communicate how serious her issues were and how depressed they made her. She ended up negotiating her own child custody agreement, and is now friends with her ex, co-parenting in a positive and supportive way to the children. A long step from leaving them without a Mother, I am very proud of her.

TALK TO SOMEONE.

TALK TO SOMEONE.

TALK TO SOMEONE.

I suggest Veteran organizations as a place to start, volunteers who have been there. Recently I read an internet article that said young veterans are rifted from the older veterans and many have said they would rather go to marathons, or sporting events, or fundraisers that are fun than to veteran groups where the old guys talk about what was called battle fatigue in their day, or other issues. I thought of a young veteran I had heard speaking at a Congressional Investigation Panel who said he too had thought, who wants to go hang out with those old guys and their stories. Then he started having some issues, and was talking to a group of older veterans and started going to their meetings. He said he now realized they too had had the same feelings and issues, and had overcome them, and it helped him heal.

My nephew came home from hospital after having been hit by a missile while gunner in a Hummer. He had joined initially because he had been promised he could go to medical school and he had a wife and small child to support, but wanted to find a way to be a doctor. When he came home, I had a talk with him, and said, when the day comes, you go talk to your Dad. You are going to find out why he was the way he was after his military service in a war zone (he had been an atomic tank mechanic electrician who had as a fun job, to defuse misfired missiles to save the tanks in Germany during the cold war). I said, you are going to find someone who was as clueless as you as to how to move forward, and be the good father and husband he wants to be, how to restore his dreams when he is too disabled to make his dreams come true at the moment. And, it will help you heal all that you blamed your Dad for, now that you are facing the same issues he did as a young husband and father just out of the service, injured inside more than out.

IF YOU ARE THINKING OF SUICIDE. TALK TO SOMEONE.

Suicide hotlines, especially those manned by other veterans may be all you need.

TALK TO STRANGERS ON THE BUS.

TALK TO STRANGERS at the train station, but TALK TO SOMEONE.

A doctor I know said when he was working in a VA hospital emergency room, a veteran came in and told the woman at the front desk he HAD TO SEE someone. She told him he had to fill out papers, and wait to be contacted. She threatened to have him arrested if he did not leave. He went to his car, and drove right on back into the waiting room. He said, NOW can you find someone to help me? That is why there are concrete and steel posts to keep cars away from the VA facility doors. BUT, I still make the calls for veterans and am greeted by that same old phone service that says inanely for minute after minute, "Don't hang up, we value your call". Maybe if they had gotten veterans together with veteran medics and found a better way to help each other faster it would have made more sense than building concrete barriers to keep out those we are by law legislated to care for since they went to war for US. Every one of us has to do something to make sure there is care and understanding when needed for our veterans. Police Departments and Emergency teams and Trauma Centers ALL have to have immediate VA contact and get the veterans in desperate need help. Some of the most successful persons in this field are volunteer veterans, and those trained by them.

I personally have made calls for distraught veterans and/or their family members to a number where the shortest wait I have ever had was 47 minutes. At one time, my phone battery would not last that long, even if fully charged. Many times I have tried to get help for a veteran, and been so irritated by the electronic message, I thought, if I had to attempt to wait 47 minutes listening to this inane message about how much they care about me, and then all kinds of messages about did I try the web site, or did I want to leave a message, because they really cared about me, it might push ME over the edge, even though it was not my problem, how much worse it must be for someone needing immediate help.

My unheeded suggestion has been to at least put the hold messages to other veterans in groups discussing the problem of wanting to die as the only viewed way to resolve something none of them knew how to deal with either, OR to have real veterans on the way through and away from the problems on suicide prevention PTSD and special volunteer lines for women veterans who have been sexually assaulted and other unique problems available on "press 1 for........" and "press 2 for ....". These groups can be trained easily, and having the problems themselves, or being family members ("press 3 for family members who do not know where to turn") or friends ("press 4 for friends who do not know where to turn") ON THE LINE to talk, or ON THE WEB to just read and listen and respond with love, not transferred calls........could be a great resource while waiting those 47 minutes. Each of those volunteers could have a list of daily local meetings for veterans, their families, friends, and first responders as well, since they have a similar high stress PTSD related suicide rate. EVERY police department should have one of these programs. Run by volunteers, and opened yesterday.

This is a place to write about care and how sad it is that veterans and family members trying to find help get a huge stone wall, and not the immediate care they need. What do they need?

IAVA in a newsletter wrote that even those who get through are often given appointments fifty or more days down the calendar. WE CAN NOT have receptionists practicing medicine. Our veterans did not tell US to wait when they were asked to put their lives on the line for our country, we need to make sure we do not ask them to wait, or qualify, or fill out paperwork, and work with a system that is not working for them, just going to give them pills and label them as mentally ill which they do not want.

The pills, shots and other medications are also a subject of discussion. On the CSPAN hearings of Congress, May 2014, it was revealed that the VA does not even return calls or offers from such prestigious hospitals and clinics as the Mayo Clinic to help our veterans. I recently called Veteran Administrations from Washington DC to our own local centers, and could not find the right person to simply send a flier to that would introduce huge free equine therapy programs of several groups across the nation to veterans and their families. Free or low cost equine therapy and therapeutic horsemanship programs, said the one woman I finally reached, SHE only referred to one place. A place that charged, and /or gave ten "free" sessions if they had raised enough money to pay themselves for doing so. In the other programs, the volunteer opportunities, and the therapy is on going, free or low cost, and in most cases has been shown to be amazingly successful. See the Documentary Soldiers and Horse Sense for an introduction to just one program. There are many others.

These volunteer phone banks can be set up locally, the VA has the technology to make sure that if a volunteer feels the need, the VOLUNTEER can ask the suicidal person or family member to talk to a supervisor at the nearest VA and get that person on the line to get immediate help. This simple and no added cost phone capability is used by collection agencies, and tele-marketing companies, we surely could utilize it to show our veterans and their families that we DO care, and CAN get them immediate help. National Homes for Heroes will send ANYONE who requests the phone bank set up for a community group the plans for $5 postage, handling and copy costs only, or you can find them free on our website. Churches, veteran's groups, community centers can set up these phone banks (Americans have the technology to allow volunteers to simply check in and have the next up call sent to their own line, and if necessary to connect to the VA itself, it is something every community with veterans, first responders and teenagers needs to add to their suicide prevention programs).

SUICIDE is a very terminal solution to what may not be a terminal problem.

Please take a moment to look at your medications if you have been thinking suicidal thoughts many of the medications being prescribed to veterans say in their televised commercials that they MAY cause suicidal thoughts, and actions, and violent behavior in some patients. IF you are taking any of these medications get to an emergency room, or your doctor NOW and get a doctor to help you.

SUICIDE is a very terminal solution to what may not be a terminal problem.

What can help?
The young actor on the Oscars just suffered through, gave it time, worked on his dreams, and became an Oscar winning actor.

Only you can decide to find dreams, and see where you are. Dr. Suess has a book for high school graduates, it says "the places you will go". Please ask for help and create new dreams. One young veteran that I love very much, since he is one of my six, or ten or forty nephews who is a veteran, recently said he was starting over, and asked that we all be supportive of him. We are. Most of the rest of us, myself included have had to start over again, and again in life, and we are not veterans, we just had the problems people get living life.

SUICIDE is a very terminal solution to what may not be a terminal problem.

When I was in my thirties one of my sisters was having relationship issues, another sister said, "Oh, at our age a broken heart lasts thirty minutes" and by my age, we can not remember what we were broken hearted about after five minutes, so go look in the refrigerator and find the keys we have been missing all day. What are they doing in there?

TALK TO SOMEONE. If you have lost a marriage, a relationship, a court custody battle, forty years of working in divorce law offices and mediation custody and property settlements lets me know that time really does heal. Get a good relationship changing book, see a family therapist to help you deal and keep on loving. One wise person said that we have to kiss a lot of toads before we find a prinz (prince or princess). A lot of toads kiss us and think we are the toads. The feeling is deep, and horrible, but you can overcome it, and one day the two of you might be standing with new partners, at a wedding, graduation, or birthday, smile at each other and know it is all worked out.

Eleven years after our divorce, my ex came over to say he wanted to apologize and that the hardest part for him to bear was that I was always so cheerful, hopeful, and happy, and when he said he wanted out of marriage, it was not fun to be a Dad and husband, that sparkle went right out of my eyes and face, and he felt horrible about it. I guess it had come back, because people often tell me, including my cancer doctors on the day I was more likely to die from the surgery than the cancer they gave me just a few days more to live with, that I am always so hopeful, so cheerful. If it was my last few minutes, why spend them sad and gloomy. In fact, I was cured, and am eleven years cancer free, so I am glad I kept cheerful and hopeful.

SUICIDE is a very terminal solution to what may not be a terminal problem.

FIND SOMEONE TO TALK TO. If the first one, or the tenth, or the hundreth do not help you find what it is YOU need to stay alive and find a new dream and not take your unique, amazing self away from those of us who DO care, keep looking, keep asking.

SUICIDE is a very terminal solution to what may not be a terminal problem.

You survived war, please do not allow peace to kill you.

SUICIDE is a very terminal solution to what may not be a terminal problem.

God bless all our veterans and their family members, our first responders, and their family members and our children, who also face large numbers of suicides in their peer group.

The author is the Training Equi-therapy Director for National Homes for Heroes/Spirit Horse II. Following a high fever disease and brain injuries that required eight years to learn to walk and talk well enough to hold hot horses for her younger son who was becoming a performance horse trainer, the author moved on and became a trainer and equi-therapy professional. Asked to create a program after Desert Storm for veterans and their families that were Court mandated due to abuse and domestic violence from PTSD, the programs have been community award winning, as well as low cost or free.

Laughter is the best medicine:

In law school, the lawyers and judges who were our professors often told lawyer jokes, or judge jokes, and even told stories from their own case work that were very funny.

One of my favorite jokes was a cartoon from the daily paper.

A Judge was shown looking down from the bench, and saying to a group of people, "THE criminals are safely back on the streets, YOU can GO now". The class was a discussion about legal ethics, and did lawyers truly have a legal ethic to guard their clients wrongs, or just their rights.

Of course the question is complex.

The point is that the law is made to protect the innocent, AND to protect the RIGHTS of all of us. IF the prosecutors, police and judges break the law, they corrupt the system.

In the movie LIAR LIAR, on the day the lawyer must tell the truth, his assistant tells him that a repeat criminal client is on the phone.......and wants "his best legal advice'. He grabs the phone and shouts. STOP COMMITTING CRIMES>

Each of us needs to think what is the best advice an expensive professional could give us!

STOP .....

What do you need to STOP, and how can you get help to do that stopping if you are not able to do it alone?

EXERPT FROM:

HOW to HEAL AMERICA and LIVE HAPPILY EVER
AFTER

Introduction:

This is book two in a series of books asking Americans to be
American, and resolve the problems of the past many years.....
but in particular the last three years of unending hate and
divisiveness.

When I was a child everyone worked on elections with their
parents, and grandparents, both parties, no bad feelings. After
the election, everyone went to big parties and celebrations
at hotels, and settled in to resolve the problems of the
community. We need to move back to times when Americans
are Americans and work on making things better, not just
immature divisive my side/your side battles that only the
overpaid politicians win. Many of the parents of my friends
were not of the same party as their spouse, or the family
grandparents.

I was talking to a friend today and asked him, please, no more
politics as usual. I have made up MY mind to be happy and do
what I can to help others find their own way to live happily and
am sure that all this negative talk is NOT going to get us there.

When I was in my Masters Degree project, we worked
on real community projects, and evaluated programs for
many school districts to help them find resolution to issues.
Whether working with families, students, police, teachers, or
administrators or all of the above, we had a rule that said,

for ANYTHING you bring in to complain about, you have to bring in an executive summary of a way to resolve the issue.

This book is about many of the issues raised in those projects and hopes to be an inspiration to parents and paid people to get the situations resolve, NO MORE divisive blaming, whining and complaining while NOTHING changes except more of the problems get worse.

There are references to some of our other work and how to create your own local programs to resolve the problems and help us ALL to live happily ever after.

WARNING:

THIS BOOK is NOT a flowers in your hair book. It is realistic look at what the world is really like and how we ALL need to admit and change things so we can live freely, justly and pursue happiness in our own ways. ALL Constitutional RIGHTS. ALL creating CONSTITUTIONAL RESPONSIBILITIES that most people do NOT think about.

LIGHTEN UP, and explore, talk to those you might not ever have thought of as having the same rights, needs, and responsibilities as you have in order for ALL of us to have those rights.

Today I was talking to someone on the phone, and forgot she was in the Philippines. I said Happy Thanksgiving, and then remembered. So I asked, does the Philippines celebrate Thanksgiving? She said no, but always wanted to experience it. I said, as I usually do, just saying what is on my mind, then have one. Then I said, they are not as pictured in movies and commercials, most of us stay in pajamas, put whatever we like to eat, or the turkey in to cook, and watch football.

Yes, I admitted, most of us have had those big formal dinners,. In my work we often have all of our volunteers do set up work, go to schools and community programs and talk to the students about veterans, and first responders, and this year the fire refugees who have not been able to return home, or their home is burned to the ground. What can we do to help everyone have happier days. After ten or twelve Thanksgiving dinners, and cooking several turkeys to drop off at the homeless shelter park for their big Thanksgiving meal, we are more than ready for our pajamas, football and whatever we have decided to eat.

One of the nicest things we learned from the veterans, and people in hospitals with serious, or terminal illness is that they can not have a Thanksgiving with family. We ask our students and volunteers to ask nursing homes, hospitals, and prisons or jails what can be donated to help the people not able to go home, feel together and cared about. One of the things the veterans and prisoners have liked the most is huge boxes of placemats made by little kids. They often put them up on the walls by their beds. Those little kid drawings of turkeys, valentine hearts, bunnies and colored eggs, or July Fourth or Veteran Day flags and thank you, along with whatever else children decide will make someone happy actually DO make a lot of people happy.

One year we had a veteran tell us his sadness because he was not able to get out of his room and even go to a gift shoppe and buy a card for his family members. He was in one of those Striker frames that keep paralyzed patients stretched and continually moving to help them heal. SOOO, we asked youth programs and classrooms to have little fundraisers and go down and buy brand new, lovely cards to donate to the social workers to give to those who needed one ......AND we raised money to put postage on all the envelopes. The social worker cried.

She was so totally happy to have something so heartfelt and so often asked for by her clients, and to be able to give it to them, given in love by others.......we felt bad, we had not wanted to make her cry. It taught us to ASK the social workers what they need and be sure they get those items. Just a box each month of snacks, and gum that can be carried around the wards and clinics, as well as the college based veteran support rooms can cost very little and make not just the social workers happy.

It led us to start little tea days, lots of bakery boxes of good things, and several teas, to have a thank you for the nurses and social workers, and techs in the hospitals and clinics. The veterans LOVED it, even it was only a signature on the huge thank you cards we had classes or Scout troops make, they felt like they were giving back. Many said it made them stop hating their staff and realize how hard it was on them as well. Every nursing home, clinic, and hospital has some administrator who LOVES giving these 45 minute thank yous to build the morale of their staff.

One of the biggest areas we were able to address was the complaint from veteran spouses and veterans with children in school that were being bullied. One child had come home several times saying the children said mean things to them. One of the usual type that does this type of bullying, a little girl with her hair pulled up so tight into braids or a pony tail her eyebrows are on the top of her head, had told the veteran child that HER Mother said her parents were NOT deployed active duty, they were just bums who left the kids off on their Grandmother. By the time one of the parents came home and became a veteran and asked us for help, we had ASKED other veterans if they had this type of complaint and designed a quick, 45 minute talk, with question and answers for classrooms, with the parents invited.

Most of the parents, and other children were shocked and angry to hear what had been going on, with the teachers not addressing the issues. IF the issues were addressed, the angry and crying veteran or active duty child was told "just forget it, there are mean people in the world". By the time we give our talk, and ALL the parents and children have a chance to say how THEY feel about this type of bullying, of active duty, veterans and first responder's children, we are able to talk about apologizing, and helping spread good and positive support rather than negative gossip and bullying for any reason.

OTHER BOOKS BY AUTHOR

Reassessing and Restructuring Public Agencies: What to do to save our Country

Carousel Horse-a teaching inclusive book about equine therapy

Spirit Horse II: Equine therapy manuals and workbooks

Could This Be Magic- a VERY short book about the time I spent with VAN HALEN

Dollars in the Streets-Lydia Caceres Edited by Author about first woman horse trainer at Belmont Park

Addicted to Dick –a healing book quasi Twelve Step for women with addiction to mean men

Addicted to Dick-2018 Edition Self help and training manual for women who allow men to torture, molest and kill their children

Books to be released:

America CAN live happily ever after: first in series of Americans resolving all the issues

America CAN live happily ever after 2: Second in series of HOW to go out and BE equal, and to part of the OF the, BY the and FOR the People our Constitution guarantees us. If the school is not teaching your children, go down and read, do math, join a science project, do lunchtime Scouting for the kids, go sit in the hallways with your smart phone and take lovely action video for the parents of kids who do not behave. More. Many suggestions from parents, and how to fundraise.

Carousel Two: Equine therapy for veterans

Still Spinning: Equine therapy for women veterans

Legal Ethics: An Oxymoron???

Friend Bird: A children's book about loneliness and how to conquer it (adults will love it too)

Kids Anonymous and Kids Jr. quasi twelve step books for and by youth and teens

12 Steps Back from Betrayal from Brothers at Arms and 12 Steps Home two quasi twelve step books and work books created by author and veterans, and author's Father for Native American and other veterans

BIG LIZ: The Leader of the Gang Racial Tension and Gang Abatement work by author

PLEASE join the tee shirt contests by checking the web sites on the books and contacting the link provided. WE love children, teens and adults helping us to give our classes free, and spread the word of our work. ALL of our work is done through education projects by our high risk youth, veterans and first responders page NATIONAL HOMES FOR HEROES/ SPIRIT HORSE II. We are just getting back to full work due to cancer of the two Directors and vehicle accidents and our stable burning down in a forest fire a couple of years ago. We promise to get more organized as we move along. 2019is our first year of taking nominations and awarding a Keiry

Equine Therapy Award. We will also need poster and tee shirt designs for that. See Carousel Horse and Spirit Horse II links to nominate a program. God bless us, as Tiny Tim said, Everyone.

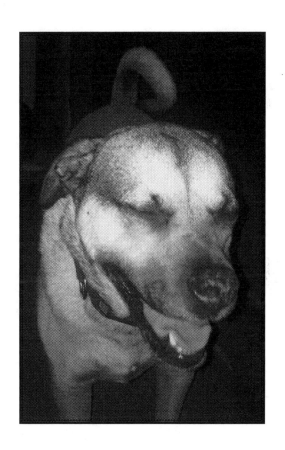

Printed in the United States
By Bookmasters